# HERALDRY
## IN ENGLAND

# HERALDRY
# IN ENGLAND

By *Richard*

ANTHONY WAGNER, *1908*

*Richmond Herald*

*The* KING PENGUIN *Books*

PUBLISHED BY PENGUIN BOOKS LIMITED

LONDON AND NEW YORK

1946

THE KING PENGUIN BOOKS

Editor: N. B. L. Pevsner
Technical Editor: R. B. Fishenden


*This Volume Published 1946*


MADE IN GREAT BRITAIN

*Text pages printed at*
THE CURWEN PRESS LTD., PLAISTOW
Set in Monotype Baskerville

*Colour Plates*
Blocks by THE ENGRAVERS GUILD LTD.
Printed by EDMUND EVANS LTD.

*Cover design by*
WILLIAM GRIMMOND

PUBLISHED BY

PENGUIN BOOKS LTD.
HARMONDSWORTH, MIDDLESEX
ENGLAND

PENGUIN BOOKS INC.
245 FIFTH AVENUE
NEW YORK

# HERALDRY IN ENGLAND

## I. *What is heraldry?*

Heraldry springs from the devices, boldly painted in bright colours, which knights in the first half of the twelfth century began to bear on their shields to identify themselves in tournament and battle. Passing from father to son these ensigns came to be thought of more as family than purely personal possessions, and so became matters of family pride and social importance. Their form and use were reduced to system. Spreading from martial to civil uses and users, they underwent much change, both of pattern, type and application. To understand these changes we must look, however briefly, at the changing background against which they took place.

## II. *Personal marks.*

Personal devices go back to the start of history, but their commonest use has not been in war, but for the civil purposes of showing ownership of property or authenticating documents. Only rarely in the long ages between the introduction of shields and the twelfth century do we find anything that looks like a personal shield device consistently used. Most military ensigns, naturally, have been collective, not personal, from the standards of the Roman legions to our own Regimental Colours and the 'New Heraldry' of Divisional Signs. The commonest and historically most continuous use of personal marks is on seals. In classical times they were used to authenticate documents and the Frankish kings preserved the custom through the dark ages. From them, when spring followed the long winter of civilization, the fashion spread to other kings and magnates in western Europe. Our own Edward the Confessor (1042–1066) started a new fashion by fastening his Great Seal to documents by a cord instead of impressing it on their surface, and took advantage of this to make it two-sided like the leaden *bulla* of the Popes. Both sides were alike and showed the king on his throne. William the Conqueror improved on this again, showing himself enthroned on one side but armed and mounted on the other. This fashion his successors have ever since followed.

At this time the normal seal device of a secular lord was his own mounted figure. For heralds it is of absorbing interest to

5

note how first one then another such little figure, on a wax seal an inch or two across, begins to show a clearly legible device upon the shield on the knight's left arm or the flag at his lance point. If his son's seal shows the same device we conclude that it has become hereditary and may safely be called heraldic. In this curiously indirect way does the new military hereditary mark, the shield of arms, link itself to the ancient civil personal mark, the seal device, so that the latter becomes our oldest evidence of the former.

Our oldest, that is, with one single, notable exception in which a written and a pictorial record combine. A chronicle tells us that, when Henry I of England knighted his newly wed son-in-law Geoffrey (called Plantagenet), Count of Anjou, in 1127, he hung about his neck a shield painted with golden lions. Now no seal showing a heraldic shield has yet been proved earlier than 1136. But this passage in the chronicle is not all. Geoffrey died in 1151 and was buried in the cathedral of Le Mans in Normandy. There is still in the museum there a portrait of him in enamel (Plate 1), made at his death or earlier, which used to hang above his tomb and shows him holding just such a shield of golden lions. As the first recorded and depicted wearer of a shield of arms and as the male ancestor of the great family of our old kings from Henry II to Richard III, it is but right that we should depict his effigy.

## III. *The origin of heraldry.*

Between 1135 and 1155 seals show the emergence of heraldry in England, France, Germany, Spain and Italy. This sudden appearance at one time over so wide a region prompts the question whether any single cause for it can be found. From long and learned discussion no certainty has issued. Some think the first crusade, by bringing knights together from many lands, may have made distinctive badges and colours needful. Others that the tournament, which then came into fashion, may have called for them, as football matches do now. Still others lay all to the charge of a great forgotten inventor. Perhaps there may be truth in all three views, and yet deeper truth outside them. The twelfth century was a great age of renewal after a long night of the mind. It was a time of invention and a time when the seed of a happy thought was carried far and quickly to take root and grow in other minds than his

6

who first thought it. But it was the age too of the great social system we call feudal; an age, that is, in which society on its secular side was held together by the personal allegiance of each man to his lord, from whom he held his land and under whom he must serve in war. If marks by which lords might be readily known were not absolutely called for by such a military and social order, certainly once invented, they would find there a ready market.

It is likewise to feudality that heraldry owes its second essential quality, its hereditary character. If service in war was the rent by which land was held, the right of inheritance by one's natural heir was an understood condition of feudal tenure. The hereditary succession to the crown of France or England was not more firmly based in law than that of the pettiest knightly house to its ancestral fee. In a world where the right to lead this man and the duty to follow that man to the wars were inherited, such an incident of service as a military device was bound to become so too. But in becoming hereditary and linking itself to feudal status and service, it as inevitably became a symbol not of the owner's identity only, but of his status too. It was knights, not their followers, who needed to be distinguished by shields and coats of arms. Therefore arms in their military aspect became in practice a mark of knightly status.

## IV. *How arms were used.*

Poetic descriptions, as well as seals, suggest that the lance flag came before the shield device and was the original 'conoissance' or cognizance. But it soon drops out. About 1160 the seal of William Fitz Empress (page 10, B), younger son of Geoffrey of Anjou and brother of Henry II, shows arms on the horse trapper, a fashion otherwise hardly known till well on in the next century. In the first half of that century arms began to be painted on the linen surcoats which knights wore over their mail. From this all armorial bearings have taken the generic name coat of arms. Geoffrey of Anjou (Plate 1) has on his pointed cap a lion like those on his shield, and later in the twelfth century we meet a similar fashion of painting heraldic devices on the front of the cylindrical helm of the day, often, but not always, repeating all or part of the shield device. From this the next step, taken in the thirteenth century,

7

was so to paint not the helm but a fan-shaped metal crest fixed to the top of it. The final stage replaced this by an actual modelled figure in wood or leather of the beast or bird or monster or whatever the device might be.

So was evolved the Crest. A modelled crest occurs as early as 1197, but they are not usual till the fourteenth century. When Edward III marched against the Scots in 1327, he surprised them by two novelties in his equipment.

Tymbris for helmis was the tane,
That thame thoucht than of gret bewte,
And alsua wounder for to se:
The tother crakkis war of wer
That thei befor herd neuir eir.

What were these two novelties 'tymbris' and 'crakkis'? They were crests and guns! We are not wont to think of them as coming in together.

Meanwhile the peaceful uses of heraldry had developed. Arms, we saw, first appear on seals not in their own right but as part of the owner's picture. But towards 1200 their growing importance is shown by their appearance as the sole or principal device (page 10, F). The large seals of barons are often two-sided (page 10, D and E), like the King's Great Seal, keeping the old fashion of the owner's mounted figure on one side, while his shield of arms fills the other. The smaller seals of lesser men commonly show the arms only. At first the shield appears alone (page 10, F). Then, as if to give it background, it is shown hanging from a tree (page 10, C). Next, it is turned at an angle and surmounted by the crested helm. This combination, of shield, helm and crest, soon became and has remained common form, and on the *lucus a non lucendo* principle the three together are called by a name that belongs to none of them, Coat of Arms. In later examples the shield is more often upright. To decorate and fill the background, seal engravers often added to the helm the cloth or mantling which was worn over it to keep the sun from overheating the metal. This too became a standard element in the design. On the great baronial or royal seals there might still remain awkward spaces between the flanks of the shield and the encircling legend. This the engravers filled with little beasts or birds or dragons, one on either side, depicted as if holding the shield up (page 10, H). By association these Supporters came thus to be regarded as an heraldic privilege of peers.

The chief civil use of arms was on seals because their use for authentication of documents gave their correctness and distinctiveness practical and legal importance. It is natural, therefore, that their influence on heraldic usage and design should be only second to that of the primary use in tournament and war. It is, however, among the many other civil uses to which heraldry was put that we must look for some of the finest and most conspicuous examples. As on seals, so on tombs it first comes in as a part of the owner's picture. The recumbent knight often holds a shield on which his arms are carved or painted or enamelled; his head may rest on a carved helm which bears his crest; and shields of his own and allied families are a common decoration for the tomb structure. After 1300 such ornament becomes profuse and often splendid; by no means on tombs only, but on panels, bosses, spandrels, corbels, walls, windows; in stone, wood, metal, paint and glass; in church, manor-house and castle; wherever an owner's or a builder's taste required it. The value of these examples as records of arms varies no less than their value as works of art. For understanding of heraldry, though commoner in the Middle Ages than now, was by no means universal. There is a comical instance in a fifteenth century copy of an older Roll of Arms (Fitzwilliam Museum, Cambridge). The painter has drawn shields to illustrate the text, but his imperfect acquaintance with the terms of blazon has made him draw shields that never were or could be.

The purely heraldic manuscripts known as Rolls of Arms would generally be the work of experts whether amateur or professional. Something will be said of these later. But arms occur as decoration, illustration or marks of ownership in many other manuscripts, and though their accuracy and quality vary greatly, these paintings and illuminations include some of the finest heraldic work.

Of other applications of heraldry to works of art and objects of use we can mention only the superb embroidery of such vestments as the Syon cope, with its fringe of shields, and the little enamelled shields which were hung on horses' harness and round heralds' necks.

A      B      C

D            E

F

G            H

V. *Arms as property.*

Distinctive marks to serve their purpose must be copyright by custom if not by law. For its first two centuries heraldry seems to have done without legal control, but the strength of the customary sanction is shown by the rarity of infringement. Down to 1300 perhaps something like fifteen hundred distinct coats had been adopted in England, and the scope for independent simultaneous adoption of the simpler designs was obviously considerable. Yet at the siege of Carlaverock in 1300 it excited general surprise when two knights, Sir Brian Fitzalan and Sir Hugh Poyntz, were both found to be bearing *Barry or and gules.*

By what, if any, machinery coordination was effected we do not know. But there is material for conjecture. Though

---

## HERALDIC SEALS

*A and C. Seal and counterseal, 1284, of Dervorguilla, daughter of Alan, Lord of Galloway, and widow of John de Balliol, founder, with her husband, of Balliol College, Oxford (Oxford Balliol Deeds, p. 363). On the seal she holds shields of (1)* Balliol [*gules*] *a voided escucheon* [*argent*] *and (2)* Galloway [*azure*] *a lion rampant* [*argent*] *crowned* [*or*], *while from trees hang those of (3)* Earldom of Chester (*of which her mother's mother was coheir*) [*azure*] *three garbs* [*or*], *(4)* Earldom of Huntingdon (*held by her mother's father and brother*) [*or*] *two piles* [*gules*]. *The counterseal shows the same four coats, but with those of* Galloway *and* Balliol *impaled in one shield.*

*B. Seal of William Fitz Empress (died 1163), son of Geoffrey Plantagenet and brother of Henry II (Northants Record Society, Vol. 4, p. 24). Shield and trapper show* A lion rampant.

*D and E. Seal and counterseal of Ralph de Monthermer. Earl of Gloucester and Hereford, 1300 (Barons' Letter to the Pope) Arms on shield and trapper,* [*or*] *an eagle displayed* [*vert*]. *Crest,* An eagle displayed [*vert*].

*F. Seal of Robert Bruce, Lord of Annandale, c. 1195 (Hunter Blair, Durham Seals, 443). A saltire* [*or*] *and on a chief* [*gules*] *a leopard* [*or*].

*G. Reverse of great seal in chancery of John Fordham, Bishop of Durham, 1382 (Durham Seals, 3142). The Bishops of Durham, as temporal lords palatine, were often shown as knights on the reverse, but enthroned as prelates on the obverse of their seals. Shield and trapper show the arms,* [*Sable*] *a chevron between three crosses paty* [*or*].

*H. Seal of John Tiptoft, Earl of Worcester, c. 1450 (Society of Antiquaries' cast). Shield, Quarterly. 1 and 4.* Tiptoft [*argent*] *a saltire engrailed* [*gules*], *2 and 3* Powis [*or*] *a lion rampant* [*gules*]; *over all, for his wife Cecily, daughter of Richard Neville, Earl of Salisbury, a shield, Quarterly 1.* Montagu [*argent*] *a fess of three fusils* [*gules*]. *2 and 3.* Monthermer [*or*] *an eagle* [*vert*]. *4.* Neville [*gules*] *a saltire* [*argent*] *and label gobony* [*argent and sable*]. *Crest,* A griffin's head [*purpure, semée of mullets or, beaked or, winged or*]. *Supporters,* two boars.

in many, perhaps most cases the reason why men chose the devices they did is lost to us, in a fair number it is clear, and in many more can be guessed at. The popular notion is that most arms are symbolic of ideal virtues, exploits in battle and the like. This is no more true of early coats of arms than of the modern signs of Army Divisions. One or two such are known. The heart in the arms of Douglas was really taken to commemorate the romantic promise, not fated to fulfilment, of Sir William Douglas to his dying master King Robert Bruce to take his heart to Jerusalem. The Pegasus in the arms of the Temple is a misdrawing of the Templars' old device of two knights riding on one horse because they were too poor to pay for two. But if there are other instances they could be counted on the fingers of one hand.

Far more characteristic of heraldry and of the mediaeval mind are the very many canting or punning coats. Some are simple and obvious. That Corbet should bear ravens, Gorges a whirlpool, Martel hammers, Trumpington trumpets, Fauconer falcons, and Swinburne boars' heads, is only natural. But others are less easily detected. It takes thought to see that each band in the Fretty coat of Maltravers has its traverse of the shield obstructed by others, that the gold dances on blue of De la Ryver depict sparkling waves, that the Dance of Sir Mauger le Vavasour makes an M or two V's or both, or that the Barry coat of Grey may depict a gré or ladder. Such interpretations rest on inference and one or two may be over subtle, but that coats were devised in this way is undoubted.

Still other coats, and among them some of the earliest, must have originated in accident or caprice. The first knights who charged their shields with bars or bends or chequers are likely to have done so for no better reason than that they made simple and distinctive patterns. But of those who bore such coats later, most will have had a better reason. 'About this time,' says Camden late in the sixteenth century, 'did many gentlemen begin to beare arms, by borrowing of their Lords Arms, of whom they hold in fee, or to whom they were most devoted. So whereas the earles of Chester bare garbs, or wheat sheafs, many gentlemen of that country tooke wheat sheafs. Whereas the old Earls of Warwick bare Chequy Or & Azure a cheveron Ermin, many thereabout took Ermin &

Chequy. In Leicestershire, & the countrey confining, divers bare Cinquefoles, for that the antient earles of Leicester bare Gules a cinquefole Ermin. In Cumberland, and thereabouts, where the old Barons of Kendal bare Argent two barres Gules and a Lion passant Or in a Canton of the second, many gentlemen thereabout tooke the same in different colours and charges in the Canton.' This copying of one man's coat by another, because of kinship, tenure or other attachment, must account for a large proportion of mediaeval coats, though the mass of instances remains to be elucidated by research. At the very start we can trace several family groups, each centring round a great man and taking arms based on his. The plain quarterly coat of Geoffrey de Mandeville, the great rebel Earl of Essex under Stephen, was copied with variations by families akin to him and to his Countess: Say, Vere, Clavering and Beauchamp. The indented chief of Ranulf Glanville, Henry II's justiciar, was taken in different forms by his Fitz Ranulf, d'Auberville and Sandwich descendants and his wife's kinsmen, the Butlers of Ireland. In Camden's instances, though there is seldom proof, tenure is a likelier reason than relationship. But much research is still needed into this heraldic reflection of the links and cross currents of feudal society. It should throw light on the social structure as well as on heraldry, genealogy and local history.

Within one family the right to the plain ancestral coat came to be looked on as belonging to the head of the house only, while his sons, brothers and remoter kindred should (but often did not) 'difference' it by more or less substantial alterations. There were many ways of differencing by altering colours and adding or exchanging charges (Plate ix). In the thirteenth and early fourteenth centuries more radical methods were in use than were possible later. For the more numerous coats grew, the harder it became to difference one without making it too like some other. So as the fourteenth century wore on, we see a fashion of less drastic differences spread downward from Royalty; first by borders and labels, plain or charged; then by small single charges, like annulets and ermine spots. Towards 1500 this fashion was systematized (by John Writhe, Garter King of Arms, it is said) into a fixed system of minute 'cadency marks', a label for the first son, a crescent for the second, and so forth, which itself has now fallen into fairly general disuse. Only in Scotland the old, drastic system of differencing by substantial alteration yet continues in full force. Camden's instances of mediaeval differencing are good ones; for example 'The Lord Clifford bare Chequy Or and Azure, a Bendlet Geules, which the elder brethren kept as long as they continued: a second sonne turned the Bendlet into a bend Geules, and thereon placed three Lionceux Passant Or, from whom the Cliffords of Frampton descended. Roger Clifford a second sonne of Walter Clifford the first, for the Bendlet took a Fesse Geules, (as the Earle of Cumberland from him descended, beareth now) and the Cliffords of Kent, branched out of that House, tooke the same with a border Geules.'

In the fourteenth century we meet with more than one kind of evidence that property in arms had acquired legal recognition. There are cases of one man granting away his arms to another, as when Lord Morley in 1347 cedes to Robert Corby the arms he had inherited from Sir Baldwin Manners. Sometimes such cessions accompany grants of land, as when William Haywode in 1404 assigns his manor of Haywode in Strathfieldsaye to John Fromonde, together with a coat of arms which appertains to the said lands. Sometimes a lord grants to one of his tenants a coat incorporating all or part of his own, just as the King of late will grant bearings out of the Royal Arms as an Augmentation of honour to a Wellington or Kitchener. Thus an Earl of Lincoln before 1311 granted one of the Scropes for his lifetime the right to charge on the bend in his coat the Earl's bearing of a purple lion; and John Touchet, Lord Audley in 1404 granted to the brothers John and Thomas Mackworth for their service to himself and their ancestors' to his, a coat combining his own two coats, *Ermine a chevron gules* for Touchet and *Gules fretty or* for Audley, into *Party indented sable and ermine a chevron gules fretty or*, which the brothers and their heirs were to bear with such differences as they themselves might choose.

The jurisdiction in armorial disputes fell, naturally enough, to the court which tried military offences, over which two military officers, the Constable and the Marshal, presided. This Curia Militaris or Court of Chivalry had its nearest counterpart in the Court of Admiralty and in its later phase had much in common with the Ecclesiastical Courts. We

14

first hear of it about 1290 and of an heraldic cause in it about 1345. Surviving records of the early Pleas of Arms are few and—apart from the three great cases, Lovel v. Morley 1386, Scrope v. Grosvenor 1389, and Grey v. Hastings 1410—very scanty. Henry VIII extinguished the office of Constable of England. But the Marshal, or Earl Marshal as he had become, maintained his Court of Chivalry and tried Peerage cases, disputes about precedence and slanders on gentility and honour as well as purely armorial causes. The Court has not been abolished but no case has been brought in it since 1734.

## VI. *Nobility and Chivalry.*

England has never had a nobility in the continental sense of a noble caste keeping its blood separate from the rest of the community's. In every generation there have been recruits from below to the governing or the educated group and at times this social turnover has been so rapid as to make a bloodless revolution. Such times were the reigns of Henry VIII, Elizabeth and Victoria. In spite or because of this we have a lively sense of aristocracy, and our national ideal of the gentleman is a sublimation of the concept of nobility for which we need not, perhaps, apologize to the rest of the world or one another.

In this peculiarly English development heraldry has played no small part. Moreover, since nearly every family, which has achieved any sort of eminence, local or national, since the later Middle Ages, has used arms with or without right, genealogical and statistical analysis of the mass of record of such use would throw more light than almost any other single study on the historical structure and texture of the English social organism. The changing fashions of heraldic composition, too, reflect not only the deeper trends of art, but changes in domestic manners and outlook.

We have seen that from being worn by individual knights, arms acquired by degrees the additional character of a badge of knightly status. It is important, however, to remember that knighthood was not then, as now, merely an honour, conferred by the sovereign in recognition of special service, but also a status which in return for the privilege of holding land imposed feudal obligations. Indeed it was a burden which those liable to it often wished to evade. In the first century after 1066, the feudal obligation kept generally its original form of personal military service. The baron held his barony on condition of supplying the King with a fixed number of armed warriors. And his tenants in their turn held their fees of him by the tenure of attending for this purpose when summoned. But as time went on and life grew more peaceful, knights became less willing to attend in person and by degrees money payments, from which the King might hire an army, were substituted. There remained a theoretical obligation on the holders of knightly fiefs to take up their knighthood when they came of age, even though they might not thereafter serve in person. This obligation Henry III and Edward I tried to enforce for military, and their successors for financial reasons, upon all who held by free tenure lands of the yearly value of £20 or more. The characteristically practical and English discrimination by a means test is to be noted. But in spite of all as time went on it came about that a large proportion of those thus theoretically bound to take up knighthood, in fact never did so. At length it became usual for a small proportion of the richer and more notable only to be required to do so individually at each Coronation. In this way under the Tudors, what had once been a widespread obligation came to be looked on as the privilege (though a costly one) of relatively few.

In much the same way the burden of attending the King's Council, imposed on the greater feudal barons largely because the King wanted money or support from them, turned by degrees into the coveted privilege of membership of the House of Lords, from which the heirs of the lesser feudal barons were shut out. These lesser barons were absorbed into the general knightly class, which at its other end did not exclude thriving citizens. The common summons to send elected representatives to Parliament is striking evidence of close and early connection between the citizens and the lesser country landowners. It was this that made our House of Commons; this that made it normal for the knight to bind his son to a trade and for the merchant to buy a manor and settle upon it; that kept the stair of social advancement open, made the manners of the court and county the nation's model; and that gave the countryman his shrewd eye for improvement of manufacture and commerce overseas. Empire, industry, democracy are all its debtors.

The feudal structure of the old English knighthood had no exact parallel abroad, but its code of manners, called Chivalry, was common to Western Christendom. It was a secular religion derived mainly from three sources: Christianity, the old northern warrior spirit and the new Provençal cult of romantic love. The first two were joined in marriage at the First Crusade, and the religious orders of knighthood, Templars and Hospitallers, were their firstborn. This older, austere knighthood fused with the Troubadours' religion of courtly love into the brilliant, unstable compound, whose bravery gilds the pages of Froissart and Malory. From this new chivalry sprang the Garter and other secular knightly orders. Tournament and heraldry were of its essence, and shields of arms have for many no meaning but what they draw from this chivalric background.

The knightly class in the later fourteenth century thus embraced both a court and camp society of knights errant, deeply tinged with chivalric notions, and a rising mercantile class, its destined successor. The peculiar social pattern, which drew no rigid line at any point between them, made it possible for the coming age to enter on its predecessor's inheritance of manners and tradition more fully than might have been thought possible. This bloodless succession of a new ruling class, linked in continuity with the old, but free to be chosen for new qualities fitting new conditions, is for better or worse a recurring and governing pattern in our history.

Henry VIII completed the thinning of the ranks of the old baronage begun by the Wars of the Roses. On their lands and those of the suppressed abbeys, his policy planted a new race of lords and gentry, drawn in part from knightly houses, and in part from new men of burgess, yeoman or servile stock. The newly granted arms of these men were at once a badge of their new standing and a pledge that the revolution they stood for would not be total. It is in this light that Henry's orders for heraldic Visitation take on so much significance. The peculiar course taken by heraldry here since Bosworth is one of many symptoms of the way in which we saved our past. Our Parliament, our Common Law, our universities, our bishops and parish priests, cities, boroughs and guilds, are legacies saved from the Middle Ages, and with them and of them is the special quality and structure of English gentry which heraldic history so perfectly reflects.

## VII. *The Heralds.*

Since classical antiquity the function of a crier and messenger in war and on State occasions has existed, and the old antiquaries not unnaturally assumed that the fourteenth-century herald was a lineal descendant of the Greek κηρυξ and the Roman *fetialis* or *praeco*. We know now that they were wrong. Heralds are first met with about 1170, not in war, but at the tournament. When a joust was to be held they proclaimed it; they cried each champion's name and prowess as he entered the lists and announced and acclaimed the victor. To these duties all their later functions can be traced. To cry a knight's name they must first know it. When his helm was closed they could only do so by his arms, and so must be learned in coat armour. Their duties at tournaments grew to keeping scores and interpreting rules and, as tournaments grew more ceremonious, to marshalling both this and other chivalric pageantry. They became a sort of professors of chivalry. From crying jousts they rose to carrying defiance and messages in war with the sacrosanct status of ambassadors. In Froissart's Chronicle of the Hundred Years War they do such service as the trusted personal servants of lords and princes. A century earlier, many—like their kinsmen and rivals, the minstrels—had been wandering free lances, hired casually for each occasion; and only the luckier had been in fixed service. But by the fourteenth century this was changed. Lords had their own heralds or pursuivants, Kings kept many, and a custom came in of baptizing them by names of office, taken from their masters' names, castles, devices or whims. Thus Chandos was Sir John Chandos' herald, Warwick the Earl of Warwick's. The King of England named Leopard Herald from his royal arms, and Windsor Herald from his royal castle. Some of the most fanciful names were given to the lower rank of heralds called pursuivants. The Earl of Northumberland's pursuivant was called Esperance from his motto, and the Duke of Gloucester's pursuivant Blanch Sanglier from his badge the white boar.

The chief heralds, like the chief of some other callings, were known as kings, and Kings of the Heralds take their place with Kings of the Minstrels, Kings of the Mercers, and Kings even of Ribalds and the Beggars. This nomenclature comes into history out of folklore, where Corn Kings and May Queens are of its kindred. From the first we find heralds called *of* or *at arms*, meaning probably that their duties were concerned with combat, whether tournament or war. Kings of heralds of arms thus came to be called more shortly Kings of Arms.

Most Kings of Arms had geographical provinces, within which they alone might marshal tournaments and perform certain other functions. In England there were at one time three provinces, those of Norroy, North of Trent, of Clarenceux, South of Trent, and of March in the West Country and Welsh marches. But March vanished before 1500 and his province was divided between the other two.

When the growing use of arms and the need for keeping them distinctive made record essential, who more naturally would keep this than the Heralds ? The oldest Rolls of Arms we know of—parchments with rows of painted shields or their written descriptions—were made about 1250, we do not know by whom (Plates 11 and 111). But we know heralds were making such rolls a century later and may infer that some at least of the first examples were their work too.

An important class of Rolls are called Occasional, because they record those present on some occasion, as a Tournament or Siege. Of these at least it is likely that heralds were the authors.

By the fifteenth century it was the Kings of Arms' duty, both in France and England, to know and register the arms of noble gentlemen within their several marches. Collections of arms arranged on a regional plan suggest that they in fact did this a century or more earlier: From this practice of heraldic survey the later Heralds' Visitations grew, and from the certifying of arms the practice peculiar to England of the granting of them by the Kings of Arms.

In 1417 important changes were made in the heraldic establishment by Henry V and his brother the Duke of Clarence. Chief of these was the institution of the new office of Garter King of Arms. This was to have a double aspect. Garter was on the one hand King of Arms of the Order of the

Garter with special duties to its Knights. But on the other he was Principal King of Arms of Englishmen, set over the existing provincial Kings, Norroy, Clarenceux and March. The manner of his institution, owing, perhaps, to Henry V's premature death, was an object lesson in how not to set up a new authority. The respective rights and duties of Garter and the Provincials were so ill drawn that they were at odds for more than three centuries after, and by their quarrels did notorious harm to the whole heraldic establishment. Its survival of such fevers is a strong testimony to the vitality of the institution.

Within thirty years of 1417 the Kings of Arms were regularly giving Patents of Arms to applicants. The form differed. Garter's patent to the Drapers' Company in 1439 (Plate VIII) merely certified that the arms which he had devised for them belonged to no one else. Others set out that Clarenceux or Norroy had satisfied himself that the applicant was a man of virtue and repute, worthy to be received among noble gentlemen, and that in token of his said gentility the said King of Arms hereby granted him such and such arms and crest to be borne by himself and his heirs. Soon after 1460 the then Clarenceux began to emphasize that he granted arms in virtue of 'the power and authority by the King's good grace to me in that behalf committed', though it was not till 1536 that the Kings of Arms' patents of appointment began to confer this power in terms.

The output of patents of arms increased steadily, with the demand, from the reign of Henry VI to that of Elizabeth, after which there began to be some falling off. The grantees were guilds and other corporate bodies, the higher ecclesiastics and all the classes of new men already named. That there was no undue exclusiveness is shown by complaints made towards 1530 that Garter had granted arms to 'bound men and vile persons not able to uphold the honour of nobless.' The distinction met with abroad between noble arms and town arms is unknown here. About the same time a minimum property qualification and a graduated scale of fees for different degrees of rank and wealth were laid down.

Many of the patents confirmed arms already in use and many coats newly assumed about this time found their way into the heralds' books not through issue of a patent, but by simple entry in the record of a local or other survey. In the third quarter of the fifteenth century these surveys or Visitations begin to give particulars of pedigree, in which heralds must long have had an interest as a means of proving gentility and title to arms. In 1530 an exceptionally violent spasm in the secular conflict between Garter and Clarenceux, in which the latter denied the former's claim to make Visitations, led to the issue by Henry VIII of an instruction which put the whole conduct of heraldic Visitations on a new and formal basis. It was laid down that only Clarenceux and Norroy might make them (personally or by deputy), each in his own province and that pedigrees as well as arms were to be entered. Powers of access to records and buildings and to prevent forcibly the bearing of unauthorized arms were conferred and exercised.

From this time down to 1686 Royal Commissions to the same effect were issued at fairly even intervals of about twenty years, and armed with the powers they gave Clarenceux and Norroy visited in recurring cycles the several counties of their provinces. The entry books of these Visitations, which are preserved at the College of Arms, contain a vast amount of genealogical and heraldic information. Their counterparts are the thousands of rolls of pedigree, in parchment or paper, emblazoned or austerely plain, given out by the heralds to those whose ancestry they entered, and to be found today in un-counted deed boxes, libraries and muniment rooms. It was the Visitation system which made the English heralds genealo-gists. They did not cease, indeed, to be ceremonial officers, but their duties in that direction gradually grew less while their genealogical activities increased. At the present day the Coronation, Opening of Parliament, Proclamations of Peace and a new King's accession, services of the Order of the Garter, and Garter's introductions of new Peers into the House of Lords are almost the only ceremonies which heralds attend. Even missions to confer the Garter on foreign kings, which preserved into the present century a memory of the heralds' employment on embassies, seem presently to have ceased for them.

As genealogists the heralds have not gone uncriticized. But, if Dethick, Cooke and Penson accepted erroneous and even fraudulent pedigrees, they did not do so with their brother heralds' approval. Their malpractices were among the causes of the violent quarrels which rent the College of Arms under Elizabeth and James I. The root of the trouble lay in the ill defined respective rights and duties of the Provincial Kings, Garter and the Earl Marshal. Constant bickering on this point made discipline and consistency hard to achieve. In the scale against its black sheep the College can, nevertheless, set a vast amount of patient, solid, unpretentious work, now of great historical use, and some dozen of the most distinguished of English antiquaries. Glover, Camden, Dugdale, Sandford, Anstis and Cokayne are names honoured where antiquaries meet.

The heralds had their first charter of incorporation, and with it a College building, from Richard III in 1484. Both, however, were shortly lost, nor was it till 1555 that Mary Tudor granted the new charter still in force and the site of the present College, with old Derby House which then stood on it. This was burnt in the fire of 1666, and for about twenty years the heralds and their records which they had saved, inhabited temporary quarters in Whitehall. Rebuilding was slow because no public funds for it were forthcoming. But by 1690 the present building was nearly complete.

With the disuse of tournaments and changes in the character of war the primary, martial use of heraldry ceased. But its civil use proportionately grew. The Tudor age was one of lavish display and decoration in which heraldry had full share. Its part in funereal solemnities was characteristic. 'Man', says Sir Thomas Browne, 'is a noble animal, splendid in ashes and pompous in the grave, celebrating nativities and deaths with equal lustre, nor omitting ceremonies of bravery in the infamy of his nature.' In the age of chivalry, if not long before, the dead knight's armour was often carried in his funeral procession and left hanging above his tomb. Some few helms and swords and gauntlets, and even tabards and shields of arms, still remain thus in our churches from the Middle Ages. When the use of these arms in war went out, their symbolic use at funerals not merely continued but increased. In the fifteenth century already the marshalling of pompous obsequies was a prerogative of the Kings of Arms, of Clarenceux and Norroy each in his own province, and of Garter for Peers and Knights of the Garter. Degrees of pomp were laid down for different ranks (Plate XIII). Where an Earl might have escucheons of taffeta, a standard six yards in length, a banner three feet square, six banner-rolls, a chief mourner supported by two Viscounts, a train borne by gentlemen, and a mourning horse, an esquire might have only escucheons of buckram, a pennon of his arms, his helm and crest, his coat of arms, a chief mourner and two assistants. The rules were last codified in 1668, just when the kind of funeral they relate to was falling into disuse. Its eighteenth-century successor, of the nodding plumes and hatchments, was by comparison a simple affair, managed by a mere upholder or undertaker, whose first appearance the heralds of the day had resented as an intrusion on their monopoly. And now even a hatchment is a black swan for rarity.

Gray's epitaph on the boast of heraldry is justified indeed.

Funeral heraldry was carried to its logical end in the decoration of the monument. Where the heraldry of mediaeval tombs is splendid in its simplicity, that of the Tudors runs to the genealogical allusiveness of many quarterings, signifying the owner's heirship of as many extinct houses. The Age of Reason put the Middle Ages out of fashion and it was its social and distinctive uses, rather than its decorativeness or romance, that then kept heraldry in some sort alive.

From the engraver and the coach painter the rising tide of the Romantic Movement and the Gothic Revival brought deliverance. Sir Walter Scott made the Middle Ages fashionable, and an early reaction on the heralds' world was a crop of peerage claims for old baronies based on the odd, unhistorical doctrine of abeyance. Absurd though some of them were, these claims gave a real impetus to feudal studies and among these to that of heraldry. Sir Harris Nicolas, on whose deep researches many of the claims were based, edited Rolls of Arms and worked closely with the heralds, among whom were some antiquaries of note. Interest in pedigree spread far and wide, and the Victorian, like the Elizabethan age, saw a vast demand for arms from the new rich and new respectable. The trade in fraudulent pedigrees did not reach Elizabethan dimensions, but there was much absurd credulity. Its most conspicuous, though not its first critic was Horace Round, an outstanding scholar, who towards the end of the last century fell on Burke's Peerage with the frustrated combativeness of an invalid. In the armorial field his friend Oswald Barron, following in the steps of Planché, Somerset Herald, with no less force than Round and more grace, drove as straight a furrow through a tangled undergrowth of ancient error. His doctrine was that only mediaeval heraldry was worth serious study and his efforts were given to disentangling its true simplicity from the modern complexities with which the current textbooks had encrusted this. The compilation, overdue but now in hand, of a complete and authoritative Dictionary of British Arms continues and builds upon his work. His controversy with Fox-Davies, an enthusiast for modern heraldry but no great scholar, was an affair of cross purposes, not wholly without comedy. It may be doubted whether Barron was right, on the one hand, in thinking true heraldry dead or Fox-Davies, on the other, in seeing the source of its current vitality in mankind's persistent snobbery. It can hardly be without significance that the most genealogically active country today is the United States of America, while the most heraldically minded, where property in arms has legal protection and cities register the arms of all classes of their citizens, is the most democratic of countries— Switzerland. Their doctrine would seem to be that heraldry and the pursuit of pedigree are valuable because they foster self respect, family unity and a feeling for the past, benefits which can and should be shared by all of us. These nations may hold that we, whose kindred bestrides the seas and who have in our College of Arms an institution unique in the whole world, do not sufficiently value our inheritance or make of it what with more imagination we might. An honest pedigree, however unambitious, and a new shield though without pretence of nobility, may warm its owner's heart, make him hold his head higher and feel himself the heir of a great tradition. He who least supposes it may be so most fully, for it has been reckoned that the English heralds in five centuries have recorded or granted arms for some 40,000 families, all of whose members are entitled to bear such arms on proof of male descent from the first owner. Of the very large number thus entitled it is likely that the great majority do not know themselves to be so, yet might with some research establish their right.

# VIII. *Blazon and design.*

A technical language for describing arms grew up slowly. Its main elements were fixed by 1250 and by 1300 practice was fairly consistent. Blazon, as it was called, was inevitably French and so remained till about 1440 when English blazon begins to come in. Latin blazon is occasionally met with at all periods, but the first attempt here to make a system of it was that of John de Bado Aureo about 1395 and the last, perhaps, that of John Gibbon, Bluemantle, in 1682.

The principle of blazon is first to name the colour of the field, then the main charge and its colour, then subsidiary charges, whether on or surrounding the main charge, and their colours. The geometrical bands and figures, which the sixteenth-century writers named *ordinaries,* have special names, *Fess, Bend, Chevron,* and the like, the chief of which Plate xv explains. Common charges may be anything in heaven, earth or wonderland, from a double-headed eagle to a trivet, but the repertory was in early days small and grew but slowly. The embodiment of old names of things in punning coats gives early blazon the combined interest of a philological museum and a crossword puzzle; while the pictures in arms of obsolete tools and the like have a good deal of antiquarian value. The simplicity of the oldest coats goes with great charm of design. Draughtsmen in the thirteenth century had often at once a freshness and a majesty of sight and touch now seldom seen. In the little art of heraldry they needed no guidance of rigid rule, but saw without telling, that it is best, in general, to paint shields in five colours only, Gold (or yellow), Silver (or white), Red, Blue and Black, with the rare addition of Green and Purple; and that generally if the field is of Gold or Silver (which we call metals) the charge should, for contrast, be of a colour, and conversely. They knew, too, that the three-cornered shield requires a certain kind of symmetry of design about its axes; that some patterns and numbers of charges look well, while others not much differing are clumsy; that heraldic drawing needs the nicest combination of boldness and discretion, and lastly that there is no expressing the thing in rules which any man will understand who cannot see the point without them.

The more numerous coats became, the more complex design and the terms of blazon were bound to grow. In the fourteenth century we pass from morning freshness to noontide splendour. When Edward III claimed the crown of France he put the French arms in a quartered shield with those of England, and the boastful gorgeousness of this famous shield is wholly typical of the time. Among the barons, too, this quartering to show unions of lordships was coming in and reached its climax in the King Maker's and other many quartered shields of the next century (page 10, H). The badges and liveries of great lords, which came in with the fifteenth century, were no other than the ensigns and uniforms of their private armies from which the England of the Wars of the Roses suffered. The Red Rose of Lancaster and White of York are but the best known Badges of many, and a fashion which began with princes had spread by the early years of Henry VIII to knights and gentry, thereafter, however, quickly dying away. Many new coats of the fifteenth century have a fanciful strangeness like nothing else in English heraldry. The early Tudor heralds, granting new coats to new men, swept these fantasies away and put in their places a crowded coarse virility of design which is rich and not unpleasing. An attractive naturalism is met with, running specially to flowers and herbs. A charged chevron between other charges and on a chief a charge between two more is a characteristic early Tudor form.

With this complexity of design came a new elaboration of terminology. Gerard Legh's 'Accedens of Armory' of 1562, laid down intricate new rules and terms of which many were soon taken into official use and are still current. Among them was the rule that the name of a tincture must not be repeated, but that instead of *Or on a chevron gules a leopard or* one must refer to the leopard as *of the field*, or *of the first*. Legh invented a host of varieties of cross with different names to mark very slight distinctions. It was left to Oswald Barron in the present century to lead a reaction towards mediaeval simplicity.

The combination of more than one coat in a shield as quarterings was begun, as has been said, to signify the union in one man of several lordships. But in the sixteenth century it took on a purely genealogical meaning and men would quarter the arms of extinct families which they represented, whether they had inherited lands from them or no. Elizabethan shields of many quarterings have great interest as exercises in genealogical research, but as art they can have only the accidental attractiveness of patchwork. In the design of single coats Elizabeth's reign, however, saw a reaction towards simplicity in new grants, as looking more mediaeval and so nobler. This lasted till the middle eighteenth century, when a fashion started for pictorial compositions wholly foreign to the genius of heraldry. Under Queen Victoria this gave place to a phase of tasteless asymmetrical overcrowding, much like that of contemporary drawing rooms. From these practices, which at their worst were nothing like universal, there has been a strong reaction.

In heraldic art there was a constant decline from Elizabeth's day to Victoria's, but growing steeper as the eighteenth century progressed. The woodcarvers of the Restoration carried into carved heraldry a fine baroque swagger much superior to most contemporary heraldic work in paint, though some of the earlier armorial porcelain (Plate XIV) and the Chippendale style bookplates have something of the same flavour. But elsewhere the tasteless preference for small, neat, insignificant charges, so beloved of heraldic stationers still, gained ever wider currency.

The crest suffered specially from loss of contact with practical reality. It is properly a composition in the round, and this should be remembered even when it is invented for no use but on paper. Yet crests have been designed in modern times which could either not be rendered in the round at all or only with much contrivance and absurdity.

Thomas Willement, the glass painter, led the Gothic Revival of heraldic design. His work is not to be despised, but has been outclassed by successors, among whom Pugin, Forbes Nixon, Dom Anselm Baker, Eve, Kruger Gray and Cobb are notable. The fillip given by Morris to decorative art generally, with its special emphasis on mediaeval excellence, had a marked effect on heraldry. The best heraldic art today can bear comparison with that of any age, but the general level, more from following bad models than want of technique, lags far behind. Nothing would help more than publication of a full and cheap series of facsimiles of the best work.

# BIBLIOGRAPHY

JAMES DALLAWAY. *Inquiries into the origin and progress of the science of heraldry in England.* 1793.

J. R. PLANCHÉ. Somerset Herald. *The Pursuivant of Arms.* 3rd edition, 1873.

J. H. PARKER. *A Glossary of terms used in British Heraldry.* New edition. 1894.

G. W. EVE. *Decorative Heraldry,* 1897; *Heraldry as Art,* 1907.

OSWALD BARRON. *Encyclopædia Britannica.* 11th edition, 1910. Article 'Heraldry'.

W. H. ST. JOHN HOPE. *Heraldry for craftsmen and designers.* 1913.

A. C. FOX DAVIES, *A complete Guide to Heraldry.* Revised edition, 1929.

C. W. SCOTT-GILES. *The Romance of Heraldry.* 1929.

A. R. WAGNER. *Historic Heraldry of Britain.* Oxford, 1939. *Heralds and Heraldry in the Middle Ages.* Oxford, 1939.

# NOTES ON THE PLATES

PLATE I.—Enamel of Geoffrey Plantagenet, Count of Anjou, about 1151 (*see* p. 6). From C. A. Stothard: *Monumental Effigies of Great Britain.* 1817, Pl. 2.

PLATE II.—Facsimile copy made about 1640 from a Roll of Arms painted and written about 1260. (Society of Antiquaries' MS. 664. Vol. I, fo. 23.) Shields of earls and barons with blazons below.

PLATE III.—*The Heralds' Roll* (College of Arms MS. B.29, p. 23, *from* Heralds' Commemorative Exhibition Catalogue, 1936, Plate xx). Shields of English lords and knights, painted about 1280, each about 1 inch by $1\frac{3}{8}$ inches. Some of the blazons

below are partly conjectural, tinctures having worn and faded.
1. *Roberd de Brus* (Bruce). Or a saltire and chief gules, a mullet
argent in dexter chief. 2. *Jon du Boys*. Argent 2 bars and a
quarter gules. 3. *Jon Comyn*. Gules 3 garbs argent. 4. *Badewyn
Wak* (Baldwin Wake). Or 2 bars and in chief 3 roundels gules.
5. *Waryn de Basyngeborne*. Gyronny or and azure. 6. *Henry de
Hastings*. Or a maunch gules. 7. *Geffrai de Lucy*. Gules crusily
3 luces or. 8. *Eumery de Lucy*. Azure crusily 3 luces or. 9. *Willem
de Sey*. Quarterly or and gules. 10. *Philip Basset*. Undy or and
gules. 11. *Willem de Brusse*. Azure crusily a lion or. 12. *Jon
Deyvile*. Or a fess gules and 3 pairs of fleurs de lys counter-
changed. 13. *Roger de Sumery*. Or 2 lions passant azure. 14. *Jon
de Vescy*. Or a cross sable. 15. *Jon Giffard*. Gules 3 lions passant
argent. 16. *Huge fiz Otes*. Or 3 bends azure a quarter ermine.
17. *John de Waus* (Vaux). Checky argent and gules. 18. *Otes de
Grantsun*. Paly argent and azure on a bend gules 3 escallops or.
19. *Jon de Seyn Jon* (St. John). Argent on a chief gules 2 pierced
mullets or. 20. *Roger de Muhaut*. Azure a lion argent. 21. *Peres
de Munfort* (Montfort). Bendy of ten or and azure. 22. *Gorge de
Cantelo*. Gules 3 leopards' heads reversed jessant de lys or.
23 *W. de Munchenesy*. Or 3 escutcheons barry of 6 vair and
gules. 24. *Robd Agulun*. Gules a fleur de lys argent. 25. *Huge
Despenser*. Quarterly argent and gules fretty or over all a
baston sable.

PLATE IV.—Illuminated miniature of Edmund Crouchback (d.
1296), Earl of Lancaster, and St. George, from Bodleian
Library MS. Douce 231, Hours of the Virgin Mary according
to the use of Sarum, *c.* 1295. Each shows his arms on shield,
surcoat, banner and the ailette on his left shoulder. Those
of the Earl are England with a label of five points azure each
point charged with a fleur de lys or (but these are much worn).

PLATE V.—Illuminated miniature of Sir Geoffrey Luttrell and his
wife and daughter-in-law, about 1340. (From the Luttrell
Psalter): Reproduced from the frontispiece of E. G. Millar's
edition by permission of the British Museum Trustees. Sir
Geoffrey is mounted and his arms, Azure a bend between six
martlets argent, appear on his surcoat, ailettes and saddle,
on the trapper of his horse, on the fan crests on his helm and
his horse, on the pennon of the lance held by one lady and on
the shield held by the other. The lady on the left, his wife
Agnes Sutton, wears a gown of *Luttrell* impaling *Sutton*, Or a
lion rampant vert. The other, Beatrice, wife of his son Sir
Andrew Luttrell and daughter of Sir Geoffrey Scrope of

Masham, wears a gown of *Luttrell* impaling *Scrope*, Azure a bend or.

PLATE VI.—Garter Stall Plate of Sir Lewis Robessart, Lord Bourchier, K.G. 1421, died 1431. Shield. Quarterly, 1st and 4th. Robessart. Vert a lion rampant or wounded in the shoulder gules. 2nd and 3rd. Bourchier. Argent a cross engrailed gules between four water bougets sable. Crest. On a torse (or wreath) azure, or and sable, a soldan's head argent, crined azure, wearing a crown or and cap gules surmounted by a Catherine wheel or and vert. Mantling. Vert bezanty. *From* St. John Hope. *The Stall Plates of the Knights of the Garter* 1348–1485, Plate XXIX. From Sir Lewis' brother descended Amy Robsart, Countess of Leicester and her niece Lucy, wife of Edward Walpole, through whom the Walpoles derive a crest based on this curious one of Robsart.

PLATE VII.—Contemporary Garter Stall Plate in St. George's Chapel, Windsor, of Ralph, Lord Basset of Drayton, Knight of the Garter 1368, died 1390. Shield. Or three piles gules a quarter (or canton) ermine. Crest. Out of a crown or a boar's head sable, tusks or. Mantling. Sable. *From* St. John Hope, *op. cit.* Plate IA.

PLATE VIII.—Heading of patent of Arms dated 10 March 1438/9 by Sir William Brugges, the first Garter King of Arms, to the Drapers' Company of London. From the frontispiece of A. H. Johnson: *History of the Worshipful Company of the Drapers of London* (by permission of the Company). The oldest known English patent of Arms. The shield is Azure three sunbeams issuing from three clouds gules (sunbursts) crowned with three imperial crowns or, alluding, as the patent says, to the Blessed Virgin, who is in the shadow of the sun yet shines with all clearness and purity, and perhaps also to the royal badge, the sunburst.

PLATE IX.—Part of a pedigree of Beauchamp with the arms of the several branches and members of the family, reproduced here to illustrate the mediaeval method of differencing (*see* pp. 13, 14) though some details need correction. From Drummond's *Histories of Noble British Families*, Vol. I, 1846, Arden, p. 9.

PLATE X.—Shields of Essex knights from a book of arms painted about 1470. (College of Arms MS. M. 10. fo. 78b; 11 by 16 inches.)

1. *Sir John Lightfote of Essex.* Gules 3 bars argent, on a bend sable 3 escallops or. 2. *Sir William Goldington of Essex.* Or 2 lions passant sable crowned and armed gules. 3. *Sir John Nevell of Essex.* Azure a lion or armed gules. 4. *Sir Thomas*

*Fynderne of Essex.* Argent a chevron between 3 crosses formy fitchy sable. 5. *Sir John Nortoft of Essex.* Gules fretty argent a fess or. 6. *Sir John Bottore of Essex.* Or a saltire engrailed sable. 7. *Sir John Mounpysson of Essex.* Argent a lion sable armed gules with a martlet or on the shoulder. 8. *Sir John Asshpolle of Essex.* Azure 3 chevrons or. 9. *Sir John Swynford of Northamptonshire.* Argent on a fess gules a boar sable armed or.

PLATE XI.—Page from a book of Visitation by Thomas Benolt, Clarenceux, 1531. (College of Arms MS. D13, fo. 42b.) *From* Heralds' Exhibition Catalogue, Pl. XXXII.
Genealogy of Thomas Fiennes. Lord Dacre of the South, with 3 shields with helms, crests and mantling. I. Fiennes. II. Fiennes quartering Dacre. III. Quarterly 1 and 4. Fiennes impaling Say. 2 and 3. Dacre impaling Multon, the whole impaling Fitzhugh (for Sir Thomas Fiennes, father of Thomas, who married Alice Fitzhugh about 1466).

PLATE XII.—Record of grants of arms made in 1530 by Thomas Benolt, Clarenceux King of Arms (College of Arms MS. L6, fo. 17). *From* Heralds' Exhibition Catalogue, Pl. XXXII. 1. Clothworkers' Company of London. Sable a chevron ermine between in chief 2 habicks argent and in base a teazle or. 2. Salters' Company of London. Per chevron azure and gules 3 covered salts argent garnished or.

PLATE XIII.—Design by Maximilian Colt for the hearse of Anne of Denmark, Queen of James I, 1619. The shields, guidons and banners on the canopy display the arms and badges of England, Scotland and Denmark; beneath it is the Queen's effigy in wax; on the four columns are the English, Scottish and Danish supporters. (College of Arms MS. I. 1, fol. 1.) *See* Mrs. Esdaile: *Illustrated London News,* 18 Aug. 1934.

PLATE XIV.—Plate from the service of armorial porcelain made about 1730 for William Pulteney, afterwards Earl of Bath (belonging to A. R. Wagner). Yung-ching period, made in China, the armorial design being sent from England. *See* Sir Algernon Tudor-Craig: *Armorial Porcelain of the Eighteenth Century,* 1925, p. 26. Shield, Argent a dance (fess dancetty) gules in chief three leopards' heads sable. Crest. A leopard's head erased sable gorged with a coronet or.

PLATE XV.—Shields drawn by Gerald Cobb to illustrate the principal terms of blazon. The dates are those of grant or first occurrence. Alternative blazons are given in brackets. I. *Thweng, c.* 1255. Argent a fess gules between three popinjays vert collared gules (collared of the second). 2. *Earl of Warwick*, *c.* 1265. Checky or and azure a chevron ermine. 3. *Washington*, *c.* 1345. Argent two bars and in chief three mullets gules. 4. *Despencer*, *c.* 1255. Quarterly argent and gules, the gules fretty or, over all a baston sable. 5. *St. Pol*, *c.* 1220. Gules three pales vair a chief or. 6. *Haberdashers' Company of London*. Barry wavy of six argent and azure on a bend gules a leopard (a lion passant guardant) or. 7. *Stanford London*, 1918. Azure a bend of five fusils (bend indented) between two crosses formy fitchy or. 8. *Deincourt*, *c.* 1255. Azure billety (semée of billets) a dance (a fess dancetty) or. 9. *St. Edward the Confessor*, *c.* 1240. Azure a cross paty between five martlets or. 10. *Dugdale*, *c.* 1600. Argent a cross moline gules and in dexter chief a torteaux (a roundel gules). 11. *Syward*, *c.* 1280. Sable a cross floretty argent. 12. *Butler*, 1568. Argent on a chief indented sable three covered cups or. 13. *De Burgh*, *c.* 1240. Lozengy gules and vair. 14. *Earl Marshal*, *c.* 1245. Per pale (party) or and vert a lion rampant gules. 15. *King of England*, 1198. Gules three leopards (lions passant guardant) or. 16. *Holland*, *c.* 1312. Azure flory (semée of fleurs de lys) a leopard (a lion rampant guardant) argent.

# GLOSSARY

Annulet, Ring

Argent, Silver (or White)

Armed, with teeth, claws, horns, beak, of a named colour, Pl. x, 2, 3, 7, 9

Azure, Blue

Badge, mark of ownership or allegiance, complete without shield or other background, p. 26

Bar, horizontal band (narrower than a *fess*), Pl. iii 2, 4, x 1, xv 3

Barry, a field divided into a number of *bars* (now always an even number), p. 11, Pl. iii 23
Barry wavy, Pl. iii 10, xv 6

Baston, narrow bend, Pl. iii 25, xv 4

Bend, diagonal band from dexter chief to sinister base, Pl. iii 16, 18, v, xi, xv 6, 7

Bendlet, narrow bend

Bendy, divided into bends, Pl. iii 21

Billety, powdered with billets, Pl. xv 8

Blazon, technical description of arms, p. 25

Bouget, water skin, Pl. vi

Cadency, p. 13

Canton, rectangular corner of the shield in dexter chief, Pl. vii

Catherine Wheel, the instrument of St. Catherine's martyrdom, Pl. vi

Charge, anything depicted on a shield of arms, p. 25

Checky, Chequy, divided into squares, like a chessboard, Pl. iii 17, xv 2

Chevron, a figure like two rafters meeting, that is with the point upwards. The so-called chevrons on British uniforms are really inverted chevrons, p. 10 G, Pl. x 4, 8, xii 1, xv 2

Chief, upper part of the shield, pp. 10 F, 26, Pl. iii 1, xv 5, 12

Cinquefoil, conventional flower of five leaves, in early heraldry often called a rose, p. 13

Coat of Arms, pp. 7, 8, 9

Crest, commonly, but quite wrongly, confused with the *shield* of arms, pp. 8, 10 D, H, 27, 30, Pl. v, vi, viii, xiv

Crined, with hair of the colour specified, Pl. vi

Crosslet, little cross, often later with the arms crossed, Pl. iii 7

Crusilly, powdered with crosslets, Pl. iii 7, 11

Dance, zigzag fess or bar, p. 12, Pl. xiv, xv

Dexter, the wearer's right side of a shield, that is the spectator's left

Displayed, spread out; the normal heraldic way of drawing an eagle, p. 10 D, E

Engrailed. Having the edge notched with a continuous series of concavities. In early heraldry a synonym for indented (q.v.), p. 10 H, Pl. vi, x 6

Ermine. Argent powdered with small black spots of varying conventional form, representing the fur of the ermine, Pl. iii 16, vii, xii 1, xv 2

Escucheon, shield, p. 10 A, C, Pl. iii 23

Fess, broad horizontal band

across the middle of the field, Pl. III 12, x 5, 9, xv 1
—— of fusils, p. 10 H

FIELD, background of a shield or charge. The colour is named first in blazoning

FITCHY, of a cross, with the base sharpened, Pl. x 4, xv 7

FLEUR DE LYS, Pl. III 12, 24, IV

FLORETTY. Cross with fleurs de lys issuing from the ends, Pl. xv 11

FLORY, powdered with fleurs de lys, Pl. xv 16

FORMY, of a cross, with spreading arms, Pl. x 4, xv 7

FRETTY, traversed by interlacing diagonal bands, Pl. III 25, x 5, xv 4

FUSIL, diamond shaped figure, p. 10 H, Pl. xv 7

GARB, Wheatsheaf, p. 12, Pl. III 3

GOBONY, divided into rectangular blocks of alternating colours, p. 10 H

GORGED, having round the neck, Pl. xIV

GRIFFIN. Monster compounded of eagle and lion, p. 10 H

GUARDANT, looking at the spectator (see *Lion*)

GULES, Red

GYRON, triangular sector of a shield

GYRONNY. Divided into gyrons, Pl. III 5

IMPALED. Divided into two by a vertical line (see *Pale*) in order to combine in one shield two coats of arms, usually those of husband and wife, p. 10 C, Pl. v, xI

INDENTED, having an edge of straight-sided teeth, Pl. xv 7, 12 (see also *Engrailed*)

LABEL, narrow bar in chief with 3 or 5 pendants; used as a difference or a mark of cadency for the eldest son, pp. 10 H, 13

LEOPARD. Lion passant guardant (q.v.), p. 10 E, Pl. xv 6, 15, 16

Leopard's head, Pl. xIV

—— reversed jessant de lys, Pl. III 22

LION, Passant, Pl. III 12, 15, x 2; Passant guardant (i.e. a Leopard), p. 10 F, Pl. xv 6, 15, 16; Rampant p. 10 A, B, C, H, Pl. I, 11, III 11, 20, v, VIII, xv 14; Rampant guardant (i.e. Leopard rampant)

LIVERY. Clothing of distinctive colours issued by a lord to his retainers, p. 26

LUCE, LUCY, Pike, Pl. III 7

MANTLING, conventional drapery hanging behind the helmet, Pl. VI, VIII, xIV

MARTLET, MERLOT, conventional small bird, usually footless, Pl. v, x 7, xv 9

MAUNCH, Sleeve, Pl. III 6

MOLINE, Cross with forked arms, in the shape of a millrind or iron which supports a millstone, Pl. xv 10

MULLET, figure like a spur rowel or star with 5 straight points, p. 10 H, Pl. III 1, 19, xv 3

OR, Gold (or yellow)

ORDINARY, an ordinary charge, one of the common geometrical figures used in arms, p. 25

PALE, vertical band, Pl. xv 5, Per Pale, xv 14, and see *Impaled*

PALY, divided into pales, Pl. III 18

PASSANT, see *Lion*

PATY, Cross with paw-shaped ends, p. 10 G, Pl. XV 9

PILE, wedge shape, issuing from the chief unless otherwise described, p. 10 A, Pl. VII

PURPURE, Purple

QUARTER, Pl. III 2, 16, VII

QUARTERING, p. 26

QUARTERLY, divided into four quarters, p. 10 H, Pl. III 9, 25, X, XI, XV 4; divided into six or more 'quarterings'

RAMPANT, see *Lion*

ROLLS OF ARMS, pp. 9, 19

ROUNDEL, Pl. III 4, XV 10

SABLE, Black

SALTIRE, X or St. Andrew's Cross, p. 10 F, H, Pl. III 1, X 6

SEMÉE, Field powdered or strewn with the charge specified, p. 10 H, Pl. III 7

SINISTER, the wearer's left side of a shield, that is the spectator's right

SUPPORTERS, pp. 9, 10 H

TORSE or WREATH, twisted band joining crest to helmet, Pl. VIII

TORTEAUX, a roundel: in modern heraldry a roundel gules, Pl. XV 10

UNDY, Barry wavy, Pl. III 9

VAIR, a conventional variegated pattern of blue and white. The name was also given to a fur of varied skins, sewn together, much used for lining garments, Pl. III 23, XV 5, 13

VERT, green

VOIDED, hollowed out, p. 10 A

# ACKNOWLEDGEMENTS

The Editor wishes to thank for permission to reproduce

     Plate II.  The Society of Antiquaries

     Plates III, X, XI, XII and XIII.  The College of Arms

     Plate IV.  The Bodleian Library

     Plate V.  The British Museum

     Plate VIII.  The Drapers' Company

I   GEOFFREY PLANTAGENET, COUNT OF ANJOU, C. 1151

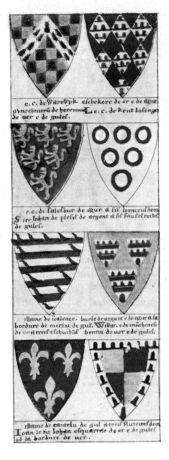

Le. c. de cestre de azur à trey gabel de or. e. c. de leicestre de gul' à lion de agent à la tone Furche.

e. c. de Ware̅w̅y̅k eschekere de or e de azur a̅ynecheuru̅ de heremm. Le. c. de kent losenge de uer e de gulef.

Le. c. de Wyncestre de gul' à set fausel lofengel de or. e. c. de hereford de azur à fil lionceus de or do une bende de argent à deul rotune de or.

e. c. de l'atelbur de azur à fil lionceul de azur. Sire Iohan de plessi de argent à fil fausel rotlet de gulef.

Le. c. de oxenford efquartele de gul' e de or

e. c. del ille de agent à yne lion de azur.

Illame de ualence. burle de argent e de azur à la bordure de merloz de gul'. Willir. e de muchenesi de or à treis eschuchu̅f bentou de uer e de gulef.

Le. c. de aubemarle de gulef à yne croyz de uer. e. c. fereres uere de or e de gul.

Illame de enntelu de gul' à treis flurettes deor. Iohn le fiz Iohan efquarirle d'g or e de gulef o̅d la bordure de uer.

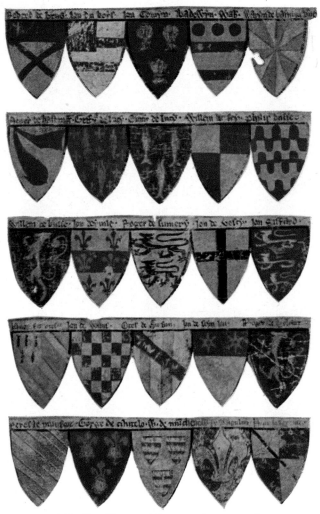

III   The Heralds' Roll of Arms, c. 1280

IV   EDMUND, EARL OF LANCASTER, AND ST. GEORGE, C. 1295

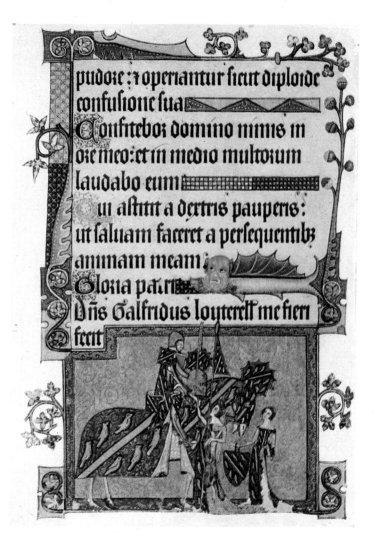

pudore : ⁊ operiantur sicut diploide
confusione sua

Confitebor domino nimis in
ore meo: et in medio multorum
laudabo eum

ui astitit a dextris pauperis:
ut saluam faceret a persequentibz
animam meam:

Gloria patri.

Dñs Galfridus louterell me fieri
fecit

V   SIR GEOFFREY LUTTRELL, FROM THE LUTTRELL PSALTER, C. 1340

VI   Garter Plate of Lewis Robessart, Lord Bourchier, K.G. 1421, d. 1431

VII  GARTER PLATE OF RALPH, LORD BASSET OF DRAYTON, K.G.
1368, d. 1390

es qui cestes presentes lettres verront ou orront humble recommendacion pleust a vous Gracie...
...Barrons le primier electeur nom et humble suiture saluure a tout la noblesse...
...our primie le tresespiritel Roy Henry le Sexisme electeur nom Roy Doungletre Fraunce...
...creatures entour grauntier et accorder a ses humbles et soialx lieges les gentz du mestier...
...et reuenue Citee de Loundres fraunchise et liberte dauoir conuocacion entre eux...
...eux pour regulauner gouuerner et auoir surueu sur la dit mestier et lan en an renoue...
...auur tout che entretenir le conduyr de tout dit corporacion les notables du mestier soubz...
...e eux de solennizier soubz dit corporacion une foiz chun du Cessaunce le lunei...
...ioit vierge Saint mere et emperisse De tout celestiel et terrestien ure tresglorious Sain...
...imperial soleile le uertus glorious Roy et sire De tout iustice che benoit Ihesu Crist...
...estier rasiesse Lune comme assentiment entre eux...
...ier estier et unfirmier nouely meistre et wardeyn...
...wont eyo... que unit estre a conuentz...
...one De blason soloin le quiel ys pourr...
...ce que a tour dit mestier entre eux du...
...nt requerez Je le suysst larrener Roy Sarrein...
...a honurable home Iohan Gedeuer le primier Me...
...cee au dit mestier Des Brodurers et aussi au...
...fratutee et contuaigne se les ay semper enseig...
...et meer Marie le quiel est en honore du so...
...coronner De troys corouns imperials Des...
...ceste lesent lire et pour recomensement...
...le quelle dit blason Je le dit larrener...

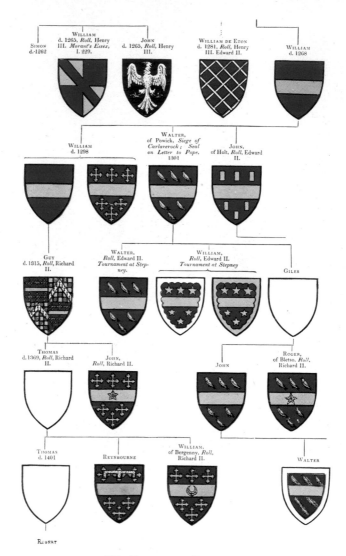

IX   PEDIGREE OF BEAUCHAMP

Sir John Lightefote of Essex    Sir Willm Goldington of Essex    Sir John Nevell of Essex

Sir Thomas Spurdene of Essex    Sir John Nortost of Essex    Sir John Gottere of Essex

Sir John Mompysson of Essex    Sir John Asshpolle of Essex    Sir John Swynford of Northampton shire

X    BOOK OF ARMS, c. 1470

Sir Thomas Jones lord Darre did marre umie doughter to the lord
Larmire and had Issheue by her of Thomas Jones unole of Thomas
Dyed his Mother keynes ..hone also he had Jhon Thomas and Marye

Sir Thomas Jones did marry Jane of one of the doughters
To the lord Sudley and had Issheue by her Thomas

XI  Heralds' Visitation, 1531

This patente was gyven & made at London by Thomas
Benette alias Clarenceux kynge at Armes of the
Sowth Easte and Weste parties of this Realme
of England vnto the Communes and occupacion of
Clothworkeres of the Citee of London deted the
xxiij daye of November in the yere of o' Lord
Ihesu Cryste a thousande ffyve hundred & xxxtie
and in the yere of the Reign of ovre moste Redoubted
Soveraign lord kyng Henry the viijth the xxijth

This patente was made & gyven at London by Thomas
Benette alias Clarenceux kynge at armes of the Sowth,
Easte & Weste parties of this Realme of England vnto
the communes and occupacion of Salters of this Citee
of London deted the viij daye of November
in the yere of ovre Lord Ihesu Cryste a thousande
ffyve hundrede and Thirtie And in the yere of
the Reign of ovre moste Dredde & Redubted
Soveraign lord kyng Henry the viijth the xxijth

XII    Arms granted in 1530 to the Clothworkers' and Salters' Companies

Coningsby Shaw

XIII  DESIGN FOR THE QUEEN'S HEARSE, 1619

XIV   Plate with the arms of Pulteney, c. 1730

XV  The terms of blazon illustrated